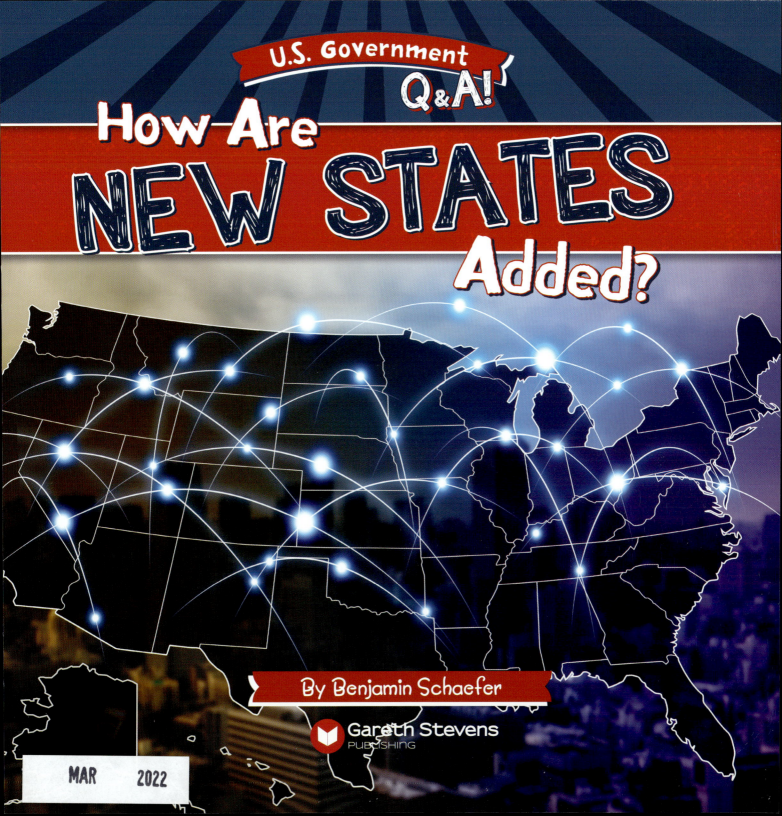

How Are NEW STATES Added?

By Benjamin Schaefer

Gareth Stevens
PUBLISHING

Please visit our website, www.garethstevens.com. For a free color catalog of all our high-quality books, call toll free 1-800-542-2595 or fax 1-877-542-2596.

Library of Congress Cataloging-in-Publication Data

Names: Schaefer, Benjamin Mark, author.
Title: How are new states added? / Benjamin Schaefer.
Description: New York : Gareth Stevens Publishing, 2022. | Series: U.S. government q & a | Includes index.
Identifiers: LCCN 2020033653 (print) | LCCN 2020033654 (ebook) | ISBN 9781538264195 (library binding) | ISBN 9781538264171 (paperback) | ISBN 9781538264188 (set) | ISBN 9781538264201 (ebook)
Subjects: LCSH: United States–Territorial expansion–Juvenile literature. | U.S. States–History–Juvenile literature.
Classification: LCC E179.5 .S3198 2022 (print) | LCC E179.5 (ebook) | DDC 973–dc23
LC record available at https://lccn.loc.gov/2020033653
LC ebook record available at https://lccn.loc.gov/2020033654

First Edition

Published in 2022 by
Gareth Stevens Publishing
29 E. 21st Street
New York, NY 10010

Designer: Andrea Davison-Bartolotta
Editor: Charlie Light

Photo credits: Cover metamorworks/Shutterstock.com; series art (paper, feather) Incomible/Shutterstock.com; series art (blue banner, red banner, stars) pingbat/Shutterstock.com; p. 5 (main) JNix/Shutterstock.com; p. 5 (inset) Wikimedia Commons/File:Stephens.jpg; pp. 5 (pins), 11 (pins), 13 (pins) Alexander Limbach/Shutterstock.com; p. 7 (background) Orhan Cam/Shutterstock.com; p. 7 (main) Jack R Perry Photography/Shutterstock.com; p. 9 (map) Invision Frame/Shutterstock.com; p. 9 (background) Prostock-studio/Shutterstock.com; pp. 11 (map), 21 (inset) courtesy of Library of Congress; p. 13 (main) Everett Collection/Shutterstock.com; p. 15 Pyty/Shutterstock.com; p. 17 f11photo/Shutterstock.com; p. 19 diy13/Shutterstock.com; p. 21 (main) Victoria Ditkovsky/Shutterstock.com.

Printed in the United States of America

Some of the images in this book illustrate individuals who are models. The depictions do not imply actual situations or events.

CPSIA compliance information: Batch #CSGS22: For further information contact Gareth Stevens, New York, New York at 1-800-542-2595.

Find us on

Contents

Words in the glossary appear in **bold** type the first time they are used in the text.

States and the Constitution

The Founding Fathers signed the **U.S. Constitution** in 1787. The United States was made up of 13 states at the time. However, the Constitution's writers wanted a way to add more states to the new Union. White settlers were moving to territories that didn't border the 13 states—land many Native Americans called home. Groups of settlers were asking for **admission** to the United States.

The Constitution's writers decided to create the New States **Clause**. It spelled out how to add new states to the country.

Government Guides

"For it is truly this circle, if we take care of her, Mother Earth, for it is true that she will always be there to take care of you!"
– Chief Oshkosh of the Menominee nation that was forced to give over 7 million acres (2.83 million ha) to the U.S. government before Wisconsin became a state.

Elizabeth "Betsy" Brown Stephens walked the Trail of Tears—the journey the Cherokee, Creek, Chickasaw, Choctaw, Seminole, and other Native people and their Black slaves were forced to make in the 1830s so white settlers could take their land.

Trail of Tears statue, Pulaski, Tennessee

The Rules

The New States Clause says a new state can't form inside a state that is already part of the United States. You can't just make your own state in Montana. Montana would have to consent, or agree. Congress would also have to agree.

What if you want to make a new state from chunks of Montana and of Idaho? Or what if Montana and Idaho want to team up and become one state? Montana, Idaho, and Congress would all have to agree in either case.

Government Guides

"The happy Union of these States is a wonder; their Constitution a miracle [an unusual event or blessing]; their example the hope of Liberty throughout the world."
– James Madison, Founding Father

Territories that belong to the United States—but aren't states yet—are ruled by Congress. This is also part of the New States Clause.

How it Happens

A territory can generally follow these steps to become a state:

First, the territory holds a **referendum** vote to see if its people want to join the Union. Second, if the vote passes and most people want to join, the territory can **petition** to Congress to be a state. Third, the territory has to make its own government or constitution. This must follow the U.S. Constitution. Finally, Congress votes on whether to pass a **resolution** accepting the territory as a state. The president finishes the process by signing the resolution.

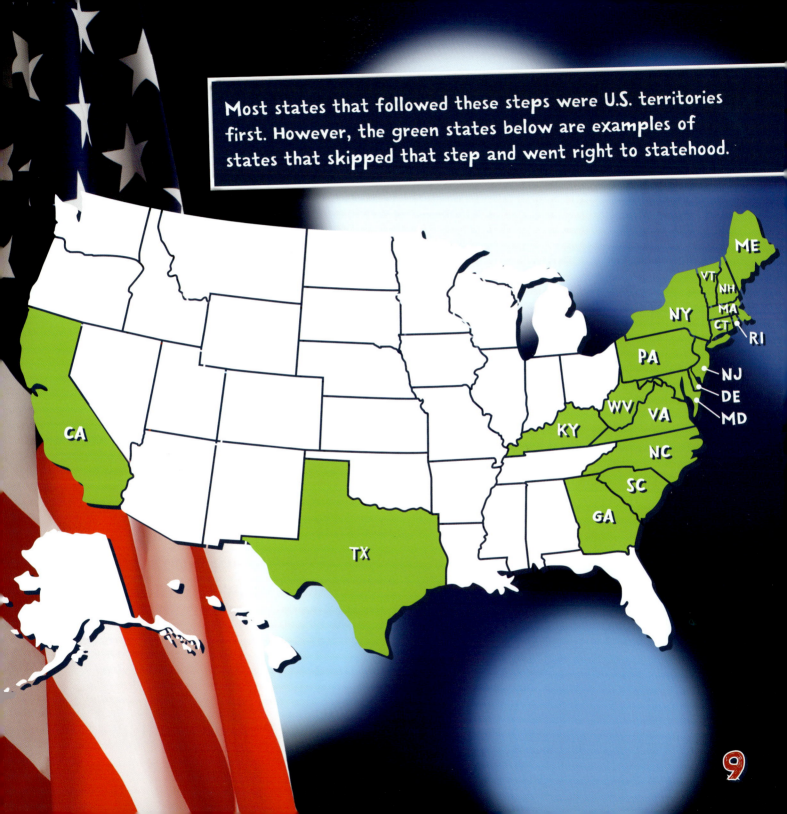

Most states that followed these steps were U.S. territories first. However, the green states below are examples of states that skipped that step and went right to statehood.

Stand on (Equal) Feet

Once a state is admitted to the Union, there is a principle called the "Equal Footing Doctrine," or the "Equality of the States." This rule says that all new states will be equal to the states that were added to the United States before them. All states will have the same rights as the original 13 states.

This principle is not in the Constitution, though. Instead, this rule has been in every state's Act of Admission. This is the last part of becoming a state.

Government Guides

James Madison was a framer, or writer, of the Constitution. He believed that western territories should only join the United States if they were treated as equals to the other states. However, the rights of all the people living in these areas were not equal.

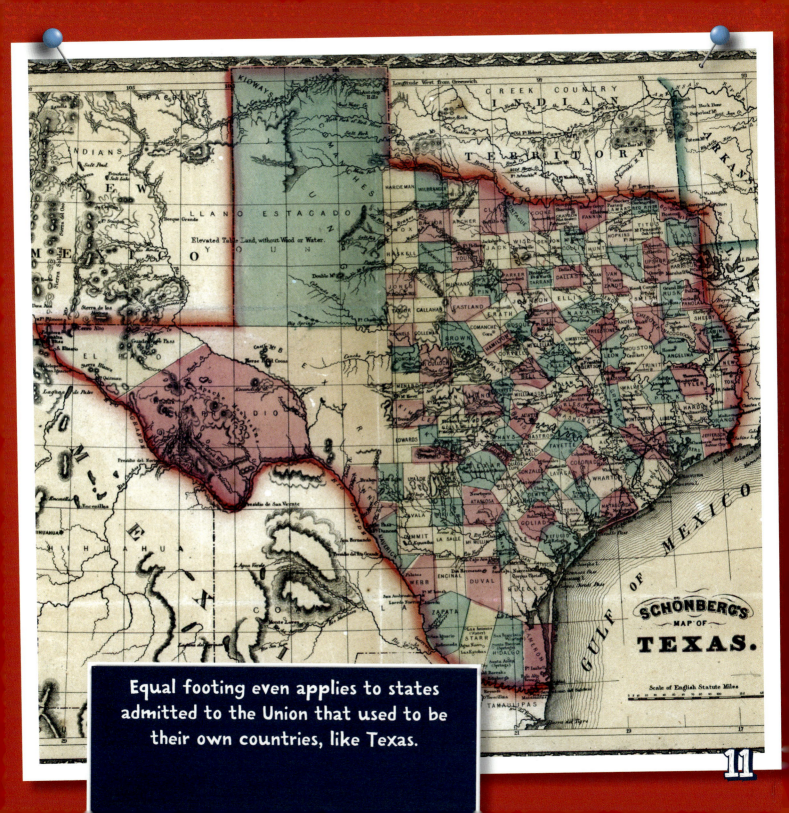

Equal footing even applies to states admitted to the Union that used to be their own countries, like Texas.

The First Expansion

New York, Virginia, Massachusetts, and Connecticut were four of the 13 founding states. They claimed they owned land to the northwest called the Northwest Territories. Congress had to decide what to do with the land. It passed the Northwest Ordinance of 1787. The ordinance, or order, said the territories would have the chance to become their own states if they followed certain steps such as having a population of at least 60,000.

The territories became Indiana, Ohio, Illinois, Michigan, and Wisconsin. Today they are together called the Midwest.

In 1803, President Thomas Jefferson bought land from France for less than 4 cents an acre, although Native Americans lived on the land. The sale was called the Louisiana Purchase. This land went on to become states too.

Manifest Destiny

During the 1800s, Manifest Destiny led white settlers to create many more states. This was the belief that the United States should expand west to the Pacific Ocean and south through Central America.

To do this, the U.S. government bought huge chunks of land, such as the Louisiana Purchase, from other countries. The Louisiana Purchase doubled the country's size. President Jefferson sent explorers Meriwether Lewis, William Clark, and soldiers to search the area. A Shoshone woman named Sacagawea and other Native Americans who lived there helped them.

Government Guides

"Whenever the people are well informed, they can be trusted with their own government."
– Thomas Jefferson,
3rd U.S. President

When Were the States Added?

1787 - Delaware, Pennsylvania, New Jersey

1788 - Georgia, Connecticut, Massachusetts, Maryland, South Carolina, New Hampshire, Virginia, New York

1789 - North Carolina

1790 - Rhode Island

1791 - Vermont

1792 - Kentucky

1796 - Tennessee

1803 - Ohio

1812 - Louisiana

1816 - Indiana

1817 - Mississippi

1818 - Illinois

1819 - Alabama

1820 - Maine

1821 - Missouri

1836 - Arkansas

1837 - Michigan

1845 - Florida, Texas

1846 - Iowa

1848 - Wisconsin

1850 - California

1858 - Minnesota

1859 - Oregon

1861 - Kansas

1863 - West Virginia

1864 - Nevada

1867 - Nebraska

1876 - Colorado

1889 - North Dakota, South Dakota, Montana, Washington

1890 - Idaho, Wyoming

1896 - Utah

1907 - Oklahoma

1912 - New Mexico, Arizona

1959 - Alaska, Hawaii

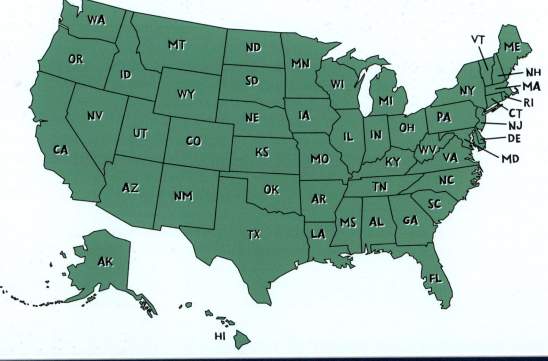

Louisiana, Missouri, Arkansas, Iowa, North Dakota, South Dakota, Nebraska, Oklahoma, Kansas, Colorado, Wyoming, Montana, and Minnesota were all created with land from the Louisiana Purchase. Many thought Manifest Destiny was important to spread U.S. government values.

Washington, DC

Washington, DC, or District of Columbia, is a special part of the country. It's our nation's capital where much of the government's work gets done. However, it's not governed, or controlled, by a state. Instead, the United States Congress has control over it. This is in the Constitution's District Clause. People living in Washington, DC, have tried to make it a state for years. The House of Representatives, Congress's lower house, passed a bill for DC's statehood in 2020. If the Senate, Congress's upper house, passes the bill, DC can become a state!

★ ★ ★ ★ ★ ★ ★ ★ ★ ★ ★ ★ ★

Government Guides

"Congress … can continue to exercise undemocratic authority [over Washington, DC] … or it can end taxation without **representation**." – Eleanor Holmes Norton, Congressional **Delegate** for Washington, DC

The United States Capitol, in Washington, DC, is where the United States Congress meets.

Puerto Rico

Puerto Rico has been a territory of the United States since 1898. It was taken from Spain as part of a deal. Some people have tried to make Puerto Rico a state. Others have tried to make Puerto Rico independent from the United States.

Puerto Ricans can't vote for president, don't have representation in the Senate, and get less government money for important things like **food stamps**. Becoming a state would change all this. In 2018, Puerto Rico's congressperson started a bill to make the territory a state. In 2020, there was a referendum on whether Puerto Rico should be a state. About 52 percent of citizens voted "yes."

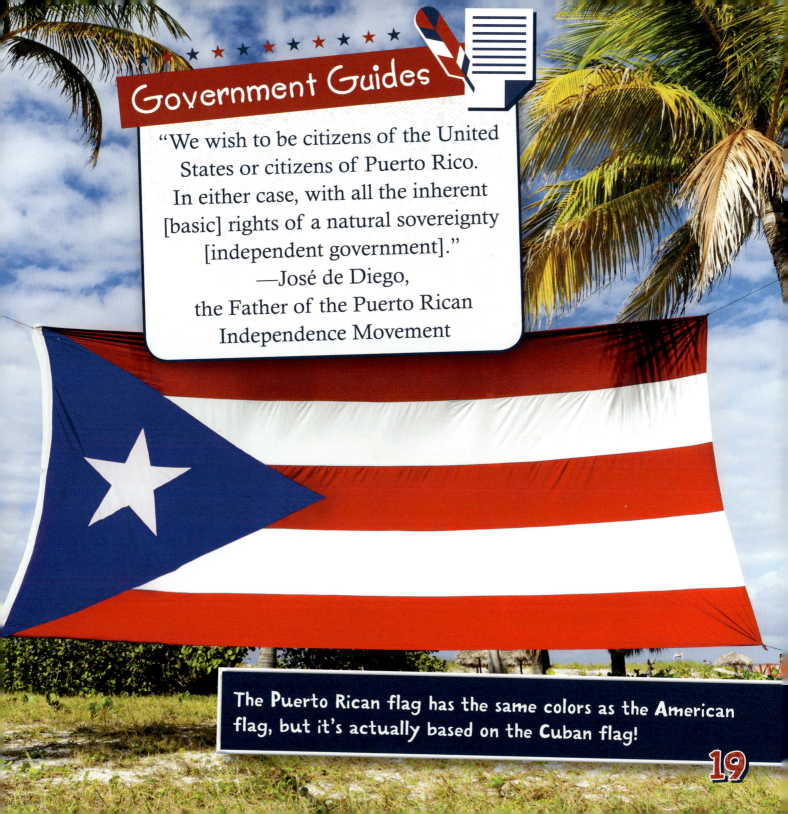

"We wish to be citizens of the United States or citizens of Puerto Rico. In either case, with all the inherent [basic] rights of a natural sovereignty [independent government]."
—José de Diego, the Father of the Puerto Rican Independence Movement

The Puerto Rican flag has the same colors as the American flag, but it's actually based on the Cuban flag!

The Newest States

The United States bought Alaska from Russia in 1867. It was a huge purchase—the land was one-fifth the size of the rest of the United States! Alaska was a territory for almost 100 years. In 1959, President Dwight Eisenhower signed a proclamation, or announcement, making Alaska the 49th state.

Hawaii was an independent nation for many years. White American settlers took it over in 1893. In 1898, the islands became a territory and part of the United States. Hawaii became the 50th state in 1959.

Think About It!

What do you think the United States government should do about Puerto Rico and Washington, DC? Should they become states? Why or why not?

Alaskan landscape

So many people thought that it was silly to buy Alaska that they called it "Seward's Folly," after **Secretary of State** William Seward who made the purchase. **A folly is a mistake.**

Glossary

admission: the action of admitting or allowing something, such as a state to join a country

clause: a part of a legal document

delegate: someone who is chosen or elected to vote or act on behalf of others

food stamps: a government program that helps people buy food

petition: a request signed by a lot of people, directed to a country or organization

referendum: the process of people or citizens voting on a law that deals with a specific issue

representation: a person or group of people that speak or act for another person or group

resolution: an official statement of purpose voted on by a group

Secretary of State: a U.S. government leader who is in charge of how the country deals with and relates to other countries

U.S. Constitution: the piece of writing that states the laws of the United States

For More Information

Books

Krajnik, Elizabeth. *The People and Culture of Puerto Rico*. New York, NY: PowerKids Press, 2018.

Platt, Christine. *Sacagawea*. North Mankato, MN: Calico Kids, 2020.

Rogers, Andrea L. *Mary and the Trail of Tears: A Cherokee Removal Survival Story*. Mankato, MN: Capstone Press, 2020.

Websites

Alaska Kids: Seward's Folly
www.alaskakids.org/index.cfm/Know-Alaska/Alaska-History/Seward's-Folly
Learn about the purchase of Alaska, the 49th state!

Brainpop Social Studies: the U.S. Constitution
www.brainpop.com/socialstudies/ushistory/usconstitution/
This resource can help you better understand all of the United States Constitution with videos and quizzes.

History: 8 Things You May Not Know—California Gold Rush
www.history.com/news/8-things-you-may-not-know-about-the-california-gold-rush
This page has great facts about how California became a state without becoming a territory first.

Index